# THE BREAKUP BOOK OF AFFIRMATIONS

# THE
# BREAKUP BOOK
# OF AFFIRMATIONS

## WORDS OF ENCOURAGEMENT TO HELP YOU MOVE ON

TIFFANY DENNY AND KIERSTYN FRANKLIN

ROCKRIDGE
PRESS

For general information on our other products and services, please contact our Customer Care Department within the United States at (866) 744-2665, or outside the United States at (510) 253-0500.

Paperback ISBN: 978-1-68539-463-9
eBook ISBN: 978-1-68539-814-9

Manufactured in the United States of America

Interior and Cover Designer: Tricia Jang
Art Producer: Melissa Malinowsky
Editor: Andrea Leptinsky
Production Editor: Jax Berman
Production Manager: David Zapanta

All illustrations used under license from Shutterstock
Author photo courtesy of Krys Mclachlan

10 9 8 7 6 5 4 3 2 1 0

TO THE LOVING PARTNERS
OUR BROKEN ROADS LED US TO,
WHO SUPPORT US IN OUR
MISSION DAILY. AND TO THE
RELATIONSHIP RECOVERY
CLIENTS AND COMMUNITY.

# INTRODUCTION

In late 2012, Tiffany was finalizing a divorce, and Kierstyn was beginning hers. We were shattered but confident in our individual decisions to move forward. Fortunately, thanks to our untimely yet timely new friendship, we were able to lean upon each other. We shared the good, the bad, and the ugly of our breakups, including the tools and resources that served us best, especially quotes, affirmations, and inspirational thoughts.

As we began our journey toward healing, we started to meet others who were just a few steps behind us. It quickly became clear that we weren't the only ones who needed this support. We took to social media in hopes of reaching the brokenhearted all over the world. As we started posting inspirational words and affirmations, our followers grew like wildfire. Our posts were being shared and saved, and messages poured in saying things like, "I needed this," "This is me!" and "I'm not alone." As the community expanded, people started asking us for support in navigating their journeys. So, we decided to become certified health and life coaches, studying relationship trauma while continuing to heal and empower ourselves and others. We then founded our company, The Relationship Recovery, through which we now coach people all over the world through relationship turmoil. The quotes and affirmations pushing our mission forward are at the heart of it all.

We found affirmations to be a powerful tool to change our clients' thought processes. When your heart is broken, affirmations can be the anchors to keep you grounded. We decided to write this book to help bring hope and comfort to as many heartbroken people as possible.

This book is intended to help you work through your breakup. It's not a replacement for mental health support. If you are experiencing debilitating depression or anxiety, we recommend that you consult a medical professional. There is no shame in getting the help you need. If you're not sure where to find help, visit the Resources section on page 127.

**_Remember, you've got this!_**

# HOW TO USE THIS BOOK

**T**hrough our coaching practice, we've seen how powerful words can heal us. We've carefully created each affirmation in this book to help shift your mindset after a breakup to compassion and self-love. Say them in the mirror, write them in your journal, read them quietly, focus on how you feel in your body, and say them until you believe them to be your truth. Use this book whichever way serves you best, whether that's reading from front to back or flipping through and picking an affirmation at random whenever you need encouragement.

I EMBRACE THE
OPPORTUNITY
TO HEAL THE
RELATIONSHIP
I HAVE WITH
MYSELF SO
THAT I MAY
HAVE HEALTHY
RELATIONSHIPS
WITH OTHERS.

TODAY, I HONOR
MYSELF, BECAUSE
I KNOW MY WORTH
COMES FROM WITHIN,
NOT FROM ANOTHER
PERSON, STATUS, OR AN
EXTERNAL SOURCE.

LOVE CONTINUES
TO ENTER MY LIFE.
I WELCOME LOVE IN ALL
FORMS, AND, ABOVE ALL,
I OFFER IT TO MYSELF.
LOVE EXPANDS AND
GROWS INSIDE ME.

SETTING BOUNDARIES FOR MYSELF IS NOT AN ACT OF SHUTTING OUT LOVE. RATHER, IT IS AN ACT OF PROTECTING THE SOIL FOR LOVE TO FLOURISH AS I SEE FIT.

I RELEASE THE MEMORIES
AND EXPECTATIONS OF MY
PREVIOUS PARTNER(S).
I RELEASE THE HURT
I FELT. I RELEASE THE
FANTASY VERSION OF US. I
EMBRACE MYSELF.

I VIEW MY NEWLY SHATTERED, BROKEN PIECES BEFORE ME AS MY BUILDING BLOCKS TO DESIGN THE NEXT CHAPTER OF MY LIFE.

I AM WILLING TO
PERCEIVE THIS
SITUATION WITH
MORE LOVE. I
CHOOSE TO BE
GRATEFUL FOR
THE LESSONS.

THE END OF A
CHAPTER DOES
NOT MEAN THE
END OF LOVE. THE
STORY IS MINE
TO WRITE; I JUST
DON'T HAVE THE
WORDS YET.

I HAVE THE AGENCY TO
SAY "YES" OR "NO" AS I
SEE FIT. DISCERNMENT
IS ONE OF THE MOST
POWERFUL WAYS TO
SHOW SELF-LOVE. TODAY,
AND EVERY DAY,
I CHOOSE MYSELF.

I GIVE MYSELF
PERMISSION TO
GRIEVE THE LOSS OF
MY RELATIONSHIP IN
MY OWN TIME SO THAT
I'M FULLY PRESENT IN
MY NEXT ONE.

I WORK TO MANIFEST
THE TYPE OF
RELATIONSHIP THAT
ALIGNS WITH MY
HIGHEST GOOD. I WILL
TRUST THE UNIVERSE
TO PROVIDE THIS.

I EXPRESS MYSELF
OPENLY AND
CONFIDENTLY. I VOW
TO NOT SHRINK
MYSELF FOR SOMEONE
ELSE'S EGO OR
COMFORT. I TAKE UP
SPACE BOLDLY AND
WITHOUT APOLOGY.

I CHOOSE TO LIVE
WITH GRATITUDE AND
COMPASSION. WHEN I
SHOW GRATITUDE, MY
HEART OPENS TO THE
LOVE AND WONDER THAT
SURROUND ME.

BY LETTING GO OF MY PAST
EXPECTATIONS, I SHOW UP
FOR THE PRESENT MOMENT
WITH HOPE, GRACE, AND
APPRECIATION.

MY LIFE IS
FULL OF EASE
AND JOY. I CELEBRATE
HOW FAR I'VE COME, AND
I AM MOTIVATED
TO SHOW UP FOR MYSELF
EACH DAY.

I KNOW I WILL FIND
LOVE AGAIN WHEN THE
TIME IS RIGHT. I KNOW
MY WORTH, AND I HAVE
MANY THINGS TO OFFER
ANOTHER.

I AM GROWING AND
CHANGING. I WELCOME
NEW THINGS INTO MY
LIFE. I FILL MY DAYS
WITH FRESH IDEAS AND
CREATIVE SOLUTIONS.

I TRUST MYSELF AS I
EMBARK ON THIS JOURNEY
TO MEND MY BROKEN HEART.
LOVE MOVES THROUGH ME
EFFORTLESSLY WITH EVERY
BREATH THAT I TAKE.

I CHOOSE TO TAKE
THIS TIME TO
DISCOVER WHAT
BRINGS ME BLISS.
I TUNE IN TO
MY INNER SELF
TO LISTEN TO
ITS NEEDS.

I UNDERSTAND THAT
I AM NOT THE FIRST
TO EXPERIENCE
THE ENDING OF A
RELATIONSHIP. I
WILL ACCEPT THE
LOVING SUPPORT OF
MY INNER CIRCLE
TO NAVIGATE THIS
CHALLENGING TIME.

BY ALLOWING MYSELF
TO MOURN THE LOSS OF
MY LAST RELATIONSHIP,
I AM FREEING MYSELF
FROM CARRYING THE
HEARTACHE WITH ME
AS I EMBARK ON NEW
ADVENTURES.

TODAY, I ALLOW MY
HEART THE TIME
IT NEEDS TO HEAL.
ALTHOUGH IT MAY
FEEL SCARRED
FROM THE PAST,
I GIVE IT SPACE
TO RECOVER AND
RECHARGE.

THE LESSONS
I'VE LEARNED
THROUGH MY
HEARTACHE ARE
INVALUABLE. WITH
EACH LESSON, I
BEGIN TO BETTER
UNDERSTAND WHAT
IT MEANS TO LOVE
AND BE LOVED.

BEING SINGLE IS
AN OPPORTUNITY
TO STRENGTHEN MY
RELATIONSHIP WITH
MYSELF. I MEET MYSELF
BY TURNING INWARD,
NOT OUTWARD. MY LOVE
FOR MYSELF GROWS.

WITH EACH DAY, MY
LONELINESS LESSENS.
I WELCOME JOY AND
LOVE INTO MY LIFE AND
MAKE ROOM FOR THE
JOURNEY I'M ON.

MY ENERGY RADIATES
HAPPINESS AND
CONFIDENCE. I SHOW UP
FOR MYSELF DAILY AND
CONTINUE TO EVOLVE INTO
A HEALTHIER, HAPPIER ME.

I FORGIVE MYSELF FOR STAYING IN A RELATIONSHIP THAT DIDN'T SERVE ME. I FORGIVE MYSELF FOR ANY HURT I CAUSED.

STEPPING AWAY FROM
RESENTMENT DOESN'T
CONDONE ANY HURT I
EXPERIENCED. IT FREES
ME TO ENTER THE NEXT
CHAPTER OF MY LIFE.

MY NEXT LOVE WILL
COME AT A TIME
WHEN I'VE OPENED
MY HEART TO MY
HIGHEST SELF. THEY
WILL COMPLEMENT ME,
RATHER THAN STIFLE
OR HINDER ME.

I WILL OFFER MY HEART TO ONLY HEALTHY FORMS OF LOVE. I HEAL SO THAT I CAN BE THE MOST AUTHENTIC VERSION OF MYSELF IN MIND, BODY, AND SPIRIT.

MY HEALING IS NOT LINEAR;
IT EBBS AND FLOWS THROUGH
DIFFERENT SEASONS OF MY
LIFE. I CONTINUALLY SHOW
MYSELF GRACE THROUGH THIS
PROCESS.

EVEN THOUGH I
MISS THE GOOD
TIMES I HAD
WITH MY EX, I
AM LIGHTER AND
CONTENT WITHOUT
THE STRESS OUR
RELATIONSHIP
CAUSED ME.

DESPITE THIS
UNSETTLING TIME IN
MY LIFE, I AM SLOWLY
LETTING THE LIGHT BACK
IN. I ALLOW MYSELF TO
FEEL MY FEELINGS.

TODAY, I CHOOSE NOT
TO LET THE HURTS
OF MY PAST KEEP ME
FROM LIVING FULLY
IN THE PRESENT. I
DESERVE WARMTH,
JOY, AND PEACE.

WHEN I LOVE MYSELF, I CAN
FREELY GIVE LOVE TO OTHERS.
TODAY, I WILL SHOW MYSELF
LOVE, COMPASSION, AND
GRACE BECAUSE I DESERVE IT.

I'M USING THIS TIME
FOR SELF-DISCOVERY,
HEALING, AND
GROWTH TO BECOME
MY GENUINE SELF. I
BELIEVE SELF-LOVE
IS MY SUPERPOWER.

I CALM MYSELF BY
TAKING A DEEP BREATH
IN. I RELEASE ALL MY
ANXIETY AS I EXHALE. I
AM AT PEACE.

I'M LEARNING HOW TO SET
HEALTHY BOUNDARIES WITH
MYSELF AND OTHERS. WHEN
I SET BOUNDARIES, I SHOW
MYSELF THE HIGHEST LEVEL
OF LOVE AND RESPECT.

FREEING MYSELF
FROM COMPARISON
ALLOWS ME TO
BRING JOY BACK
INTO MY LIFE. I
MAKE SPACE FOR
EMPATHY AND
FORGIVENESS
FOR MYSELF
AND OTHERS.

DESPITE THE HURT I'VE ENDURED, I CHOOSE TO KEEP MY HEART SOFT. I EMBRACE LETTING MY PAINFUL EXPERIENCES TEACH AND GUIDE ME, NOT HARDEN ME.

IN ORDER FOR ME TO
HAVE INNER PEACE, I
FORGIVE THOSE WHO
HAVE WRONGED ME. I LET
LOVE AND LIGHT IN WHEN
I LET GO.

TODAY, I HONOR MYSELF,
EVEN THOUGH OTHERS
MAY NOT HONOR ME.
MY LOVE FOR MYSELF
IS MORE IMPORTANT
THAN ANY OTHER LOVE I
WILL HAVE.

I SET FREE ANY
EXPECTATIONS OF HOW
LONG IT SHOULD TAKE
ME TO HEAL FROM THIS
BREAKUP. INSTEAD, I
WILL MAKE MORE ROOM
FOR SELF-COMPASSION
AND SELF-LOVE DURING
MY HEALING JOURNEY.

I SEE EVERY CHALLENGE
I FACE AS AN
OPPORTUNITY TO GROW
AND IMPROVE MYSELF. I
KNOW THAT GREATNESS
COMES FROM SOME
OF LIFE'S HARDEST
LESSONS.

TODAY, I ABANDON OLD
HABITS AND PATTERNS
SO I CAN LIVE FREE OF
THE BELIEFS THAT HAVE
HELD ME BACK FROM
LIVING AUTHENTICALLY.

I CHOOSE TO OPEN
MY HEART AND
LET LOVE IN. I'M
LEARNING TO
TRUST AGAIN, AND I
DESERVE ALL THAT
AWAITS ME.

I DESERVE PARTNERS WHO APPROACH ME WITH PATIENCE, KINDNESS, AND COMPASSION.

I CHOOSE TO STAY
PRESENT. LIVING
IN THE PAST WILL
KEEP ME STUCK, AND
WORRYING ABOUT THE
FUTURE DOES NOT
SERVE ME.

SETBACKS DO NOT DEFINE ME; THEY NUDGE ME INTO NEW AWARENESS. I AM CONNECTED TO MY LIFE, AND I MOVE FORWARD WITH THE NEW KNOWLEDGE I HAVE GAINED.

I RELEASE WHAT DOESN'T SERVE ME ANYMORE AND GIVE MYSELF PERMISSION TO HEAL. I NO LONGER HOLD ON TO NEGATIVE THOUGHTS AND BELIEFS.

MY INTUITION
IS MY GREATEST
STRENGTH. MY
GREATEST GUIDE
TO LOVE IS WITHIN
ME, AND IT WILL LEAD
ME TO THE HAPPY LIFE
I DESERVE.

DESIRE AND
CONTENTMENT CAN
COEXIST WITHIN
ME. I CAN DESIRE A
RELATIONSHIP WITH
SOMEONE I HAVEN'T
MET AND BE CONTENT
WITH BEING SINGLE
RIGHT NOW.

HAPPINESS CAN COME
FROM WHERE MY
HEART BROKE. I STEP
FORWARD INTO THE
UNKNOWN TO RECLAIM
THE JOY THAT'S IN
MY HEART.

LOVING MYSELF WILL
HELP BREAK THE
CYCLE OF UNHEALTHY
RELATIONSHIPS. I AM
COMPASSIONATE AND
GENTLE WITH MYSELF
THROUGH ALL PHASES
OF MY LIFE.

I OPEN MY HEART TO
WELCOME AUTHENTIC
CONNECTIONS. THE MORE
MY LOVE FOR MYSELF
GROWS, THE MORE
I CAN OPEN MYSELF
TO OTHERS.

THERE IS MORE LOVE
WITHIN ME THAN
I EVER IMAGINED
POSSIBLE. LOVE
FLOWS OPENLY TO
ME AND FROM ME. I
FEEL LOVE CRASHING
OVER ME.

EVERYTHING I
NEED TO BE HAPPY
COMES FROM WITHIN
ME. I WELCOME NEW
RELATIONSHIPS, BUT
I DO NOT COMPROMISE
THE RELATIONSHIP I
HAVE WITH MYSELF.

BECAUSE I HONOR
MYSELF, I WILL NOT
SELF-ABANDON FOR
ANYONE ELSE. I WALK
AWAY AT THE FIRST
SIGN OF ANYTHING
LESS THAN I DESERVE.

I USE THIS TIME TO
GAIN CLARITY ABOUT
EXACTLY WHAT LOVE
MEANS TO ME AND WHAT
MY STANDARDS FOR
RELATIONSHIPS ARE.

THIS PRESENT MOMENT
IS ALL THAT MATTERS. BY
EMBRACING WHERE I AM
TODAY, I WILL GET TO WHERE
I WANT TO BE IN MY LIFE.

THE CHALLENGES I HAVE
ENCOUNTERED HAVE
MADE ME STRONGER.
THEY INSPIRE ME TO BE
THE BEST VERSION OF
MYSELF DAILY.

THERE IS NO
HEARTBREAK THAT I
CANNOT OVERCOME.
I FEEL MY EMOTIONS
AND ALLOW MYSELF
TIME TO PROCESS
THEM. I WILL
RELEASE THEM
WHEN I'M READY.

BY STANDING
BRAVELY AS MY
AUTHENTIC SELF,
I ATTRACT PEOPLE
INTO MY LIFE WHO
CELEBRATE AND
SUPPORT ME RATHER
THAN MAKE ME
FEEL SMALL.

LOVE IS ALREADY MINE.
I FEEL IT EVERY DAY
IN EVERYTHING I DO. I
SHOW LOVE TO ANYONE
AND EVERYONE WHO
COMES INTO MY LIFE.

MY ROMANTIC
HISTORY DOES NOT
DEFINE MY FUTURE
RELATIONSHIPS. I AM
INFLUENCED BY MY
DATING HISTORY, BUT
I AM NOT DEFINED BY
IT. IT HELPS ME MAKE
BETTER DECISIONS
ABOUT WHO I ALLOW
INTO MY LIFE.

I CHOOSE TO PUT MY
NEEDS FIRST SO THAT
I CAN SHOW UP FULLY
FOR MY FUTURE SELF
AND BECOME WHO I AM
INSPIRED TO BE.

THE RELATIONSHIPS
IN MY LIFE BRING
ABUNDANCE AND JOY. I
AM GRATEFUL FOR ALL
THE LOVE I ALREADY
HAVE SURROUNDING ME.

MY HAPPINESS IS
MY PRIORITY. I GIVE
MYSELF PERMISSION
TO SAY NO TO WHAT
DOESN'T SERVE ME AND
ONLY CHOOSE THINGS
THAT BRING ME JOY.

BEAUTIFUL RELATIONSHIPS OCCUR BETWEEN PEOPLE WHO ARE CONFIDENT IN WHO THEY ARE. I AM IN TUNE WITH WHO I AM AND WHAT I WANT.

I ATTRACT AND EMBRACE
NOURISHING AND GENUINE
RELATIONSHIPS EVERY
DAY. I VALUE EACH OF THEM
FOR WHAT THEY BRING TO
MY LIFE AND WHAT THEY
TEACH ME.

IF ALL I CAN DO IS
EXIST TODAY, THAT
IS ENOUGH. WHEN
THINGS FEEL VERY
HEAVY, I EMBRACE
THAT IT'S OKAY TO
SIT IN STILLNESS.

THIS BREAKUP IS A
SMALL PART OF MY
STORY. I CHOOSE
TO BEGIN THE NEXT
CHAPTER OF MY LIFE
AND EMBRACE NEW
BEGINNINGS.

MY HEART IS OPEN TO
NEW POSSIBILITIES.
EVERY DAY I FEEL MYSELF
GETTING STRONGER,
AND I AM EXCITED ABOUT
WHAT MY FUTURE HOLDS
FOR ME.

I AM AT PEACE WITH MY
PAST. I GIVE MYSELF
PERMISSION TODAY TO
START WITH A CLEAN
SLATE, AN OPEN HEART,
AND AN OPEN MIND.

I CHOOSE TO MAKE MY
MENTAL WELL-BEING
MY PRIORITY. I
REPLACE CRITICAL
AND OVERWORRYING
THOUGHTS WITH
PEACEFUL ONES AND
WELCOME TRUE AND
LASTING CHANGE.

I MAKE DECISIONS THAT SUPPORT MY SELF-VALUE AND SELF-WORTH. I LISTEN TO MY INTUITION AND FOLLOW GUIDANCE COMING FROM MY HEART.

MY CONTENTMENT
IS NOT RELIANT ON
EXTERNAL THINGS
OR OTHER PEOPLE;
IT COMES FROM
WITHIN. I CHOOSE
TO LIVE MY LIFE
UNAPOLOGETICALLY
AND AUTHENTICALLY.

I MANAGE THE WAY I
REACT TO MY CURRENT
SITUATION. I'M FOCUSED
ON KEEPING A POSITIVE
ATTITUDE WHILE CONTINUING
TO HEAL AND GROW.

CHANGE CAN BE SCARY,
BUT IT'S A POWERFUL
TEACHER. I'M OPEN
AND WILLING TO MAKE
ROOM FOR DIFFERENT
EXPERIENCES TO
CONTINUE TO TEACH ME
NEW THINGS.

THE WAY I TALK TO
MYSELF IS CRUCIAL FOR
SELF-HEALING. SINCERITY,
COMPASSION, AND PEACE
ARE ALL PARTS OF MY
INNER DIALOGUE.

STARTING OVER ALLOWS
ME TO KNOW WHAT I
REALLY WANT. AS I MOVE
FORWARD, I REBUILD
TRUST IN MYSELF TO
MAKE GOOD DECISIONS.

I AM WORTHY OF
BEING LOVED EVEN
WHEN I AM HURTING.
I CAN ACCEPT
MYSELF EVEN
THOUGH I AM NOT
PERFECT. I EMBRACE
MY IMPERFECTIONS.

MY WORTH IS NOT
BASED ON HOW OTHER
PEOPLE LOVE ME
BUT ON HOW I LOVE
MYSELF. I PRACTICE
DAILY TO LOVE AND
HONOR MYSELF.

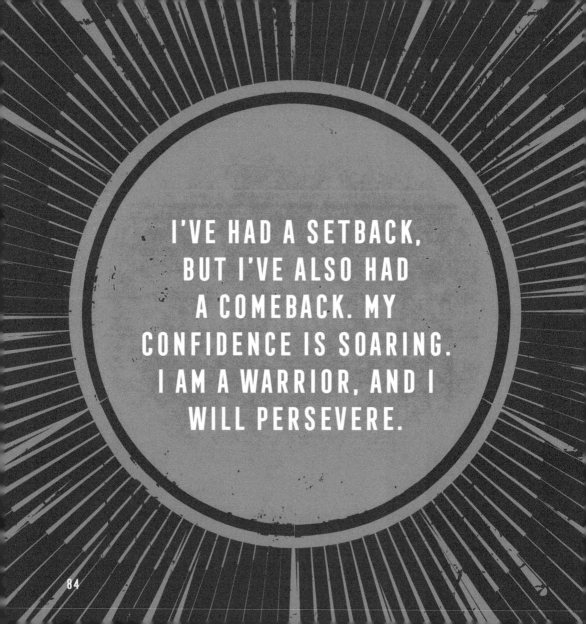

I'VE HAD A SETBACK, BUT I'VE ALSO HAD A COMEBACK. MY CONFIDENCE IS SOARING. I AM A WARRIOR, AND I WILL PERSEVERE.

FEARING AN UNCERTAIN
FUTURE DRAINS ME OF
ENERGY AND ROBS ME
OF LIVING FULLY IN THE
PRESENT. I FREE MYSELF BY
ACCEPTING THE UNKNOWN.

I AM STARTING TO
FEEL MORE LIKE
MYSELF AGAIN.
I'M INTENTIONAL
ABOUT SELF-CARE
AND SELF-LOVE. THE
BETTER I BECOME, THE
BETTER I ATTRACT.

I AM NOT RESPONSIBLE FOR THE ACTIONS AND BEHAVIORS OF ANOTHER PERSON. I'M ACCOUNTABLE FOR MY OWN ACTIONS AND BEHAVIORS AND FOR HEALING MYSELF.

EVERY LIFE
EXPERIENCE GIVES
ME THE OPPORTUNITY
TO GROW AND BECOME
WISER. I WELCOME
NEW BEGINNINGS
AND LET GO OF OLD
ENDINGS.

I AM RESILIENT ENOUGH
TO RECOVER FROM
ANY CHALLENGING
SITUATION. I SHOW UP
FOR MYSELF EVERY DAY,
EVEN WHEN I DON'T FEEL
LIKE IT.

AS I EMBARK ON MY
SELF-LOVE JOURNEY, I'M
DISCOVERING THINGS
ABOUT MYSELF. I CHOOSE
TO COME FROM A PLACE
OF CURIOSITY RATHER
THAN JUDGMENT.

BY LIVING IN
HARMONY WITH MY
DESIRES, VALUES,
AND GOALS, I BUILD
A MORE AUTHENTIC
LIFE, OPENING MYSELF
UP TO MEANINGFUL
RELATIONSHIPS.

RELEASING THE
DISAPPOINTMENT OF
THE PAST ALLOWS
ME TO EMBRACE THE
POSSIBILITIES OF A
BRIGHTER TOMORROW.
I MOVE FORWARD WITH
LOVE, COURAGE, AND
CONFIDENCE.

I EMPOWER MYSELF TO TAKE
MY TIME TO GET CLEAR ON
THE RELATIONSHIP I DESIRE.
I TRUST THAT THE RIGHT
PERSON WILL ENTER MY LIFE,
BUT I DON'T PUT PRESSURE ON
MYSELF TO FIND THEM.

WHEN I FOCUS ON THE GOOD RELATIONSHIPS IN MY LIFE, THEY MULTIPLY. I HAVE MORE OPPORTUNITIES TO BUILD CLOSE AND MEANINGFUL CONNECTIONS WITH OTHER PEOPLE.

THE TOOLS I NEED
TO OVERCOME
THE OBSTACLES
IN MY LIFE ARE
AVAILABLE TO ME
NOW. I WELCOME
THESE OBSTACLES
WITHOUT FEAR.

PEOPLE'S CHOICES
ARE NOT MINE TO
CONTROL. I RELEASE
THE IMPULSE TO
CONTROL WHAT
I CANNOT AND
INSTEAD FOCUS ON
WHAT I CAN.

I AM GENTLE WITH
MYSELF DURING
THIS TRANSITION. I
REALIZE I AM GROWING
AND BECOMING
MORE OF WHO I AM
SUPPOSED TO BE.

BY GETTING OUT OF
MY HEAD AND INTO
MY HEART, I AM
MORE CONNECTED
TO MYSELF AND
TO OTHERS.

MY NEXT RELATIONSHIP
WILL BE OPEN, HONEST,
AND FULL OF LOVE,
JOY, SAFETY, AND
ABUNDANCE. I CHOOSE
TO LET GO OF FEAR AND
EMBRACE LOVE.

LOVING MYSELF FIRST
IS THE BEST CHOICE
I CAN MAKE FOR THE
PEOPLE AROUND ME.
THE MORE FULFILLED
I AM, THE MORE LOVE
I SHARE.

BEING ALONE IS
HARD AT TIMES,
BUT I CAN DO
HARD THINGS. THE
CHALLENGING
MOMENTS MAKE
ME STRONGER.

I REFUSE TO OVERTHINK MY SITUATION BUT INSTEAD CHOOSE TO FEEL MY ANSWER. MY HEART WILL LEAD ME TO CLARITY, AND I TRUST ITS WISDOM.

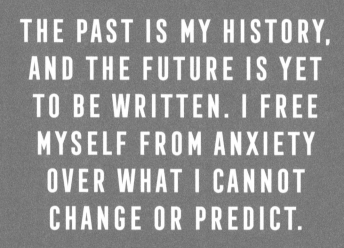

THE PAST IS MY HISTORY, AND THE FUTURE IS YET TO BE WRITTEN. I FREE MYSELF FROM ANXIETY OVER WHAT I CANNOT CHANGE OR PREDICT.

BY RELEASING NEGATIVE
FEELINGS ABOUT THE
PAST, I AM MORE AT PEACE,
WHICH GROUNDS ME IN A
HAPPIER EXISTENCE.

I KNOW WHAT LOVE MEANS TO ME. MY PATH IS CLEAR, AND I AM READY FOR LOVE IN ALL FORMS AND RELATIONSHIPS, NOT JUST ROMANTIC LOVE.

MY ENERGY IS FOCUSED
ON THE PRESENT.
I DEVOTE MYSELF
ENTIRELY TO THIS
MOMENT. EVERYTHING
I NEED TO BE HAPPY IS
AVAILABLE RIGHT NOW.

THOSE I ACCEPT INTO MY LIFE WILL COMPLEMENT ME, NOT DEFINE ME. I AM WORTHY AND WHOLE AS I AM AND WILL ENTER INTO RELATIONSHIPS THAT ARE IN ALIGNMENT WITH THIS TRUTH.

MY HEALTHY
BOUNDARIES FREE
ME TO HONOR WHAT
I WANT MOST. MORE
GENUINE, NOURISHING,
LOVING RELATIONSHIPS
WILL COME FROM
THIS CHOICE.

IRRATIONAL THOUGHTS
AND NEGATIVITY KEEP
ME FROM BEING THE
PERSON I DESIRE TO BE.
I CHOOSE TO FOCUS ON
THE GOOD.

I DARE TO WALK AWAY FROM
RELATIONSHIPS THAT DO
NOT ALIGN WITH MY GOALS.
I ATTRACT PEACE AND
SECURITY INTO ALL ASPECTS
OF MY LIFE.

NEW BEGINNINGS COME
TO ME IN ABUNDANCE. I
RELEASE ALL PHYSICAL
AND MENTAL CLUTTER
TO FREE UP SPACE FOR
NEW PEOPLE, PLACES,
AND THINGS.

I STRIVE TO MAKE
PROGRESS IN HEALING
MYSELF EVERY DAY.
I LOOK FOR EVERY
OPPORTUNITY TO MAKE
PROGRESS TOWARD MY
PERSONAL GROWTH
AND HAPPINESS.

EVEN THOUGH THIS
RELATIONSHIP HAD TO COME
TO A CLOSE, I TRUST THAT
EVERYTHING WILL WORK OUT
FOR MY HIGHEST GOOD.

I CHANGE MY
LIMITING BELIEFS
INTO EMPOWERING
ONES. I CHOOSE HOW
I WANT TO FEEL, AND
TODAY I CHOOSE TO
FEEL CONFIDENT AND
POWERFUL.

THIS JOURNEY I'M ON IS SHAPING ME INTO THE BEST VERSION OF MYSELF. IT'S TEACHING ME THAT I'M THE ARCHITECT OF MY LIFE.

EVERY DAY I FIND
THINGS TO BE
GRATEFUL FOR
ABOUT THIS SEASON
OF MY LIFE. WHEN
I ENCOUNTER
ROADBLOCKS, I
TURN THEM INTO
STEPPING-STONES.

REGARDLESS
OF WHAT LIFE
THROWS AT ME,
WITH STRENGTH,
I CONTINUE MY
EVOLUTION INTO
THE BEST VERSION
OF MYSELF.

TODAY, I SURRENDER
ALL OF MY DOUBTS
AND FEARS. I
UNDERSTAND THAT
MY FEELINGS AND
ANXIOUS THOUGHTS
ARE ONLY TEMPORARY.

I PRIORITIZE PEOPLE
WHO BRING ME PEACE AND
RESPECT ME. I WILL LIMIT
MY TIME AND ENERGY
FOR PEOPLE WHO DO THE
OPPOSITE.

SELF-LOVE AND
SELF-CARE ARE MY
TOP PRIORITIES. I
SHOWER MYSELF WITH
COMPASSION, LOVE,
RESPECT, AND POSITIVE
THOUGHTS AS I GROW
AND HEAL MYSELF.

EVEN THOUGH LIFE
IS HARD SOMETIMES,
I ACKNOWLEDGE
THE GOOD THINGS IN
MY LIFE AND WILL
LET THEM BE THE
FOUNDATION OF MY
FUTURE.

I WORK WITH INTENTION TOWARD OPENING MY HEART AND MIND TO THE IDEA THAT I AM LOVED AND CAN RECEIVE LOVE.

I AM CONFIDENT
THINGS WILL WORK
OUT EVEN IF I AM
STRUGGLING RIGHT
NOW. I TRUST THAT
EVERYTHING IS WORKING
TOWARD MY LONG-TERM
HAPPINESS.

EVERY DAY
IS ANOTHER
OPPORTUNITY TO
FEEL HAPPY AND
MORE CONFIDENT IN
MYSELF. I PRACTICE
RELAXATION AND
DEEP BREATHING
DAILY TO HELP ME
CALM MY MIND.

I AM LOVE.
I AM LOVE.
I AM LOVE.

# RESOURCES

## EMERGENCY SERVICES

The National Domestic Violence Hotline at 1-800-799-7233 serves victims of domestic violence and those at risk.

## BOOKS

*You Are a Badass: How to Stop Doubting Your Greatness and Start Living an Awesome Life* by Jen Sincero.

## WEBSITES

Psychology Today offers a database of therapists and psychiatrists for those in need of mental health support. Search for a provider at PsychologyToday.com/therapists.

The Relationship Recovery offers an array of coaching services: The Relationship Recovery Podcast, coaching programs, courses, and retreats. Visit TheRelationshipRecovery.com to learn more.

# ACKNOWLEDGMENTS

Thank you to our clients, followers, and all those who have allowed us to walk with them on their healing journeys. Thank you to Rockridge Press for giving us this opportunity. Thank you to our parents who believed we were capable, even before we believed it. Thank you to our amazingly supportive family and friends. To our loves, TJ and Tim; we couldn't do this without your support. This is all for our children, Colton, Carson, Noah, Jake, Libbey, Luke, Grey, and CeCe, in hopes of healthier relationships for generations to follow.

# ABOUT THE AUTHORS

 For the past ten years, Tiffany Denny and Kierstyn Franklin have been helping people worldwide heal from relationship turmoil through their company, The Relationship Recovery. After personally experiencing relation-ship turmoil and not finding the resources they needed, they curated a program with proven techniques to help people heal after a broken heart through mindset change.

CPSIA information can be obtained
at www.ICGtesting.com
Printed in the USA
BVHW021922180822
644954BV00019B/471

9 781685 394639